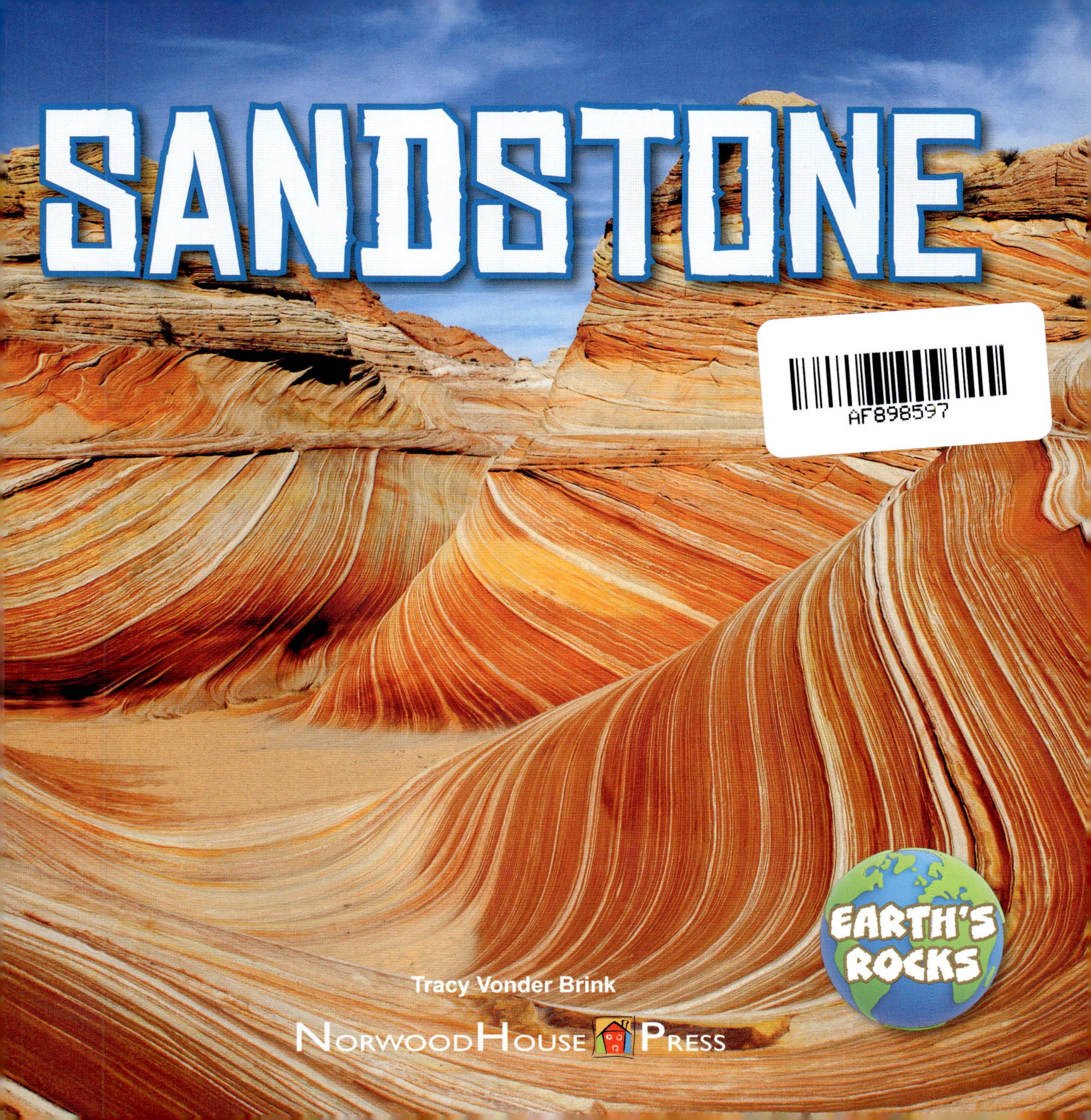

SANDSTONE

EARTH'S ROCKS

Tracy Vonder Brink

NORWOOD HOUSE PRESS

Cataloging-in-Publication Data

Names: Vonder Brink, Tracy.
Title: Sandstone / Tracy Vonder Brink.
Description: Buffalo, NY : Norwood House Press, 2027. | Series: Earth's rocks | Includes glossary and index.
Identifiers: ISBN 9781978580176 (pbk.) | ISBN 9781978580183 (library bound) | ISBN 9781978580190 (ebook)
Subjects: LCSH: Sedimentary rocks--Juvenile literature. | Geology--Juvenile literature. | Rocks--Juvenile literature.
Classification: LCC QE471.V66 2027 | DDC 552.5--dc23

Published in 2027 by
Norwood House Press
2544 Clinton Street
Buffalo, NY 14224

Designer: Rhea Magaro
Editor: Kim Thompson

Photo credits: Cover, p. 1 Tu Le/Shutterstock.com; p. 3 Khatsola Oksana/Shutterstock.com; p. 4 Kavic.C/Shutterstock.com; p. 5 Alexandre.ROSA/Shutterstock.com; p. 6 J. background/Shutterstock.com; p. 7 sirtravelalot/Shutterstock.com; p. 8 BlueRingMedia/Shutterstock.com; p. 9 Agorca/Shutterstock.com; p. 10 Nick Greaves/Shutterstock.com; p. 11 cathrynahoyt/Shutterstock.com; p. 12 Ulderico Granger/Shutterstock.com; p. 13 NipaArts/Shutterstock.com; p. 14 VGV MEDIA/Shutterstock.com; p. 15 ddg57/Shutterstock.com; p. 16 Goldilock Project/Shutterstock.com; p. 18 Ivan Ventura/Shutterstock.com; p. 19 Mikhail Sedov/Shutterstock.com; p. 21 K.L. Kohn/Shutterstock.com;

Printed in the United States of America

CPSIA compliance information: Batch #CSNHP27: For further information contact Norwood House Press at 1-800-237-9932.

TABLE OF CONTENTS

WHAT IS SANDSTONE?

Rocks make up many things in the world, from tall mountains to the deep seafloor. All rocks are made of **minerals**. They are put into three main groups based on how they form.

Types of Rock

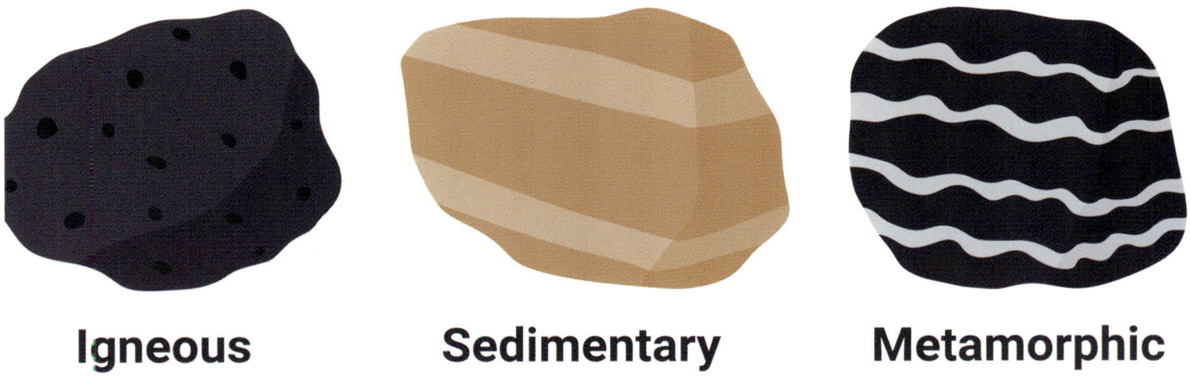

Sedimentary rocks are formed from bits of other rocks. Sandstone is a sedimentary rock.

Sandstone begins as layers of sand. You can see these layers in the rock.

The color of sandstone depends on what kind of sand made it. Sandstone can be red or orange. It can be white or tan. Some even looks pink.

HOW DOES SANDSTONE FORM?

Like all rocks, sandstone forms during Earth's rock cycle.

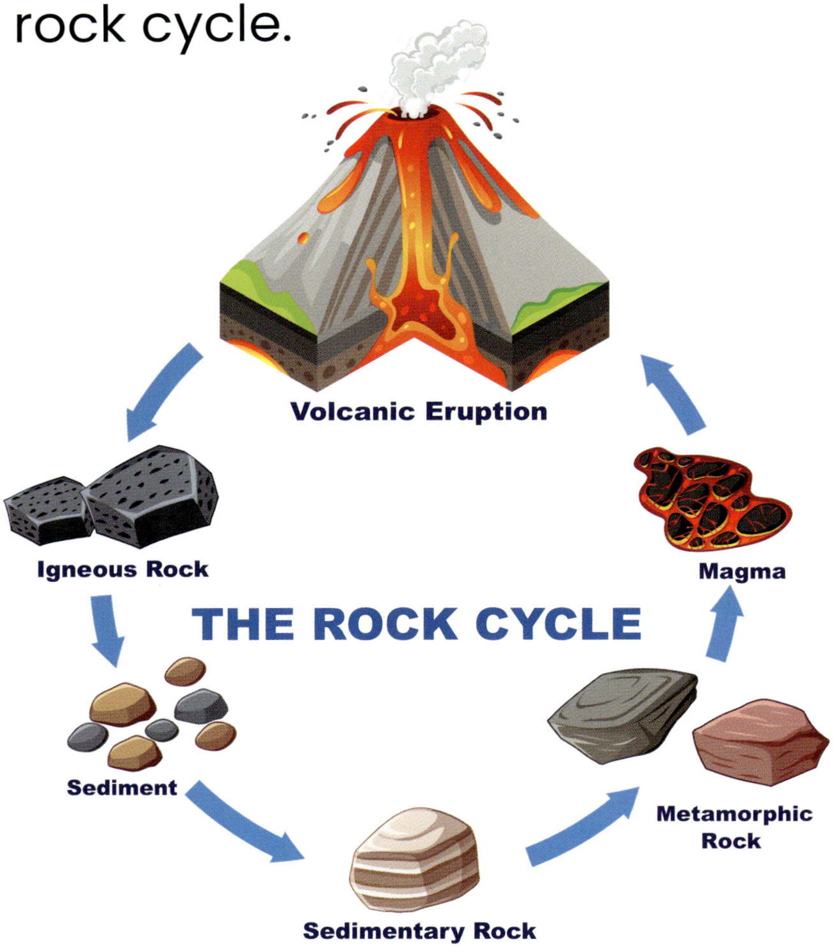

Sandstone starts with rocks on or near Earth's surface. They often contain the mineral quartz. **Weathering** breaks off tiny **grains** of sand from these rocks.

Wind, rain, and ice carry the grains into bodies of water. This process is called **erosion**.

The sand grains pile up at the bottom of rivers, lakes, and oceans. Over time, thousands of layers of **sediment** are put down.

The layers become so heavy that they **compress** the sand. This **compaction** squishes the grains closer together.

Water flows around the layers. It carries minerals that act like cement. They make the sand stick together.

The minerals also harden the stuck-together sand. Over millions of years, it turns into rock.

WHERE IS SANDSTONE FOUND?

Sandstone is one of the most common sedimentary rocks. It is found around the world. It makes up at least one-tenth of all the sedimentary rocks in Earth's **crust**.

Some underground sandstones act as **reservoirs**. They hold important natural resources like oil, gas, and water.

The Navajo Sandstone spreads across parts of Nevada, Arizona, Colorado, and Utah in the United States. It formed from the largest known desert on ancient Earth! Parts of the Navajo Sandstone are nearly 200 million years old.

HOW IS SANDSTONE USED?

Sandstone has been used to build everything from castles to churches. The outer walls of the White House in Washington, D.C., are made of sandstone.

Sandstone is also used in floors and patios. It can be crushed to make bricks and concrete.

Sandstone is a useful rock. It is common, but it is also beautiful. You can see it at the Grand Canyon and other magnificent places around the world.

GLOSSARY

compaction (kuhm-PAK-shuhn): a process in which sand, dirt, clay, or small rocks are pressed together over time so that the space between the pieces gets smaller

compress (kuhm-PRES): to press or flatten something

crust (kruhst): the hard outer layer of Earth where people, plants, and animals live

erosion (i-ROH-zhuhn): the process by which bits of rock are carried away by wind, water, or ice

grains (graynz): very small pieces of something

minerals (MIN-ur-uhlz): solids that form naturally in Earth and that do not come from an animal or plant; sandstone contains minerals such as quartz and mica

reservoirs (REZ-uh-vwahrz): places where resources are kept in store; natural underground reservoirs are cavities in rock where water, oil, and other materials collect

sediment (SED-uh-muhnt): bits of natural materials, such as sand or shells, that settle in layers

weathering (WETH-ur-ing): the process by which natural forces break rocks into smaller pieces

THINKING QUESTIONS

1. How are rocks put into groups?
2. What does sandstone look like?
3. How does erosion help form sandstone?
4. What is compaction?
5. Describe some ways people use sandstone.

INDEX

ABOUT THE AUTHOR

Tracy Vonder Brink is always curious about the world around her. She loves to make facts and true stories fun and has written many books for kids. Tracy lives near Cincinnati, Ohio, and enjoys reading, hiking, and playing with her two rescue dogs.